UNDENIABLE CONFIDENCE

Empower Yourself For Success

Hasheem Francis &
Deborah Francis

For information about reprints rights, translation, or bulk purchases, please contact Deborah Francis at info@BTPPublish.com, or you can write to BTP Publishing at P.O Box 552, Plymouth, FL 32768. www.BTPPublish.com

UNDENIABLE CONFIDENCE
Authors: Hasheem Francis & Deborah Francis
Cover design by: BTP Publishing Group
Edited By: BTP Publishing Group
ISBN: 978-0615859538
Published by: BTP Publishing Group Plymouth, FL (www.BTPPublish.com)

TABLE OF CONTENTS

INTRODUCTION

"Opportunities are constantly flowing past you in the stream of life unless you reach out and grab them! If you don't know what you are looking for, how can you get it?" -- **Claude M. Bristol**

With half a billion innovative books being published every year, there is absolutely no scarcity of resources to assist you in developing yourself into a confident individual with a positive attitude and influence.

Undeniable Confidence is a book which will give you an insight into this important attribute which has made men and women enter the books of history.

In this book, all the principles and factors associated with confidence will be discussed. It has been proven that confidence can help you realize your God-given potential in life. *Undeniable Confidence* will give you an exceptional understanding of confidence—what it is and how you can use it to bring a positive change into your life. It will help you overcome worries such as Can I manage? Am I the best? What will I do? What will happen?

The best asset that every human being has is his or her mind, and the mind is the only recollection source that cannot be completely filled. It is full of as much knowledge as the owner places inside of it. The brain is filled with a great deal of information which can either make you poor or enrich you, depending on the information with which you feed it. The kind of information you load into your mind will determine what you will achieve in life. The mind operates on a system of garbage in and garbage out.

Be cautious about how you think and what you think, because your life will be shaped by the thoughts that you have meditated upon. What you frequently feed your mind is going to impact you negatively or positively. The images that you have in your mind will have power over your life.

We are transformed by what we have in our mind. Our life will turn out to be that in which our mind is being fixed. The type of things that we consistently download into our mind will either make us feel rejected or accepted in life.

Among the greatest functions that an individual has is the development his or her mind. The more you develop your mind, the better off you will be. The power of the mind can only be abused when you do not effectively put it to good use. All of the technologies that are used these days, as well as the legacy that has been left by a number of inventors, became a reality due to individuals making use of their mind. If you develop your mind, your mind will in turn develop your life. The individual who fails to develop their mind is the poorest individual on the earth.

Enhance your mind by building it up with essential information which will be applicable in life and in turn, it will improve you.

"If you think you can, you can. And if you think you can't, you're right" --- **Henry Ford.**

No wonder Henry Ford, a very respected and confident man, put the wheels of modern automobiles in motion and also acted as a powerful catalyst in the 20th century economy and society.

In today's world, there is such a strong emphasize on the importance of self-confidence; that most people have no choice but to spruce up their confidence levels or they will be left far behind in the rat race and never be able to rise above it.

How to Stay Positive in Spite of the Negativity Around You

It is human nature to have down times where we feel discouraged, depressed and listless. The difference lies in how quickly we choose to get over those things that are holding us back or making us feel less than our personal best. And that, I believe, is the key: being able to get past the downtimes in one's life as quickly as possible and remain at your best, moving forward in continuous improvement.

Remember, self-improvement is a hands-on project. Without ongoing implementation of the new ideas we learn, try as we may, we are not going to miraculously wake up one day as changed people. No, we've got to act on those ideas and bits of advice we learn.

Here is a saying by Zig Ziglar (he has such a simple yet powerful way of getting his point across): "People often say motivation doesn't last. Well, that may be true but neither does bathing—that's why we recommend it every day."

Understanding the need to attend to motivation and inspiration on a daily basis can lead to a more positive life. Let's look at it another way: You wake up and you pretty much have a clean slate. In most cases, your day is fresh—neither overly negative nor positive. That being the case, then wouldn't it stand to reason that importing (i.e. reading, listening, reciting, meditating, viewing, etc.) positive thoughts first thing in the morning and throughout your day could do wonders towards reprogramming the way in which you see your world?

Read Henry Ford's quote, *"If you think you can, you can. And if you think you can't, you're right,"* several times a day. Also, choose to read from an inspirational book or listen to inspirational songs at least three times a day. In addition, immediately balance any negative experiences with something positive.

Given the events of most people's days, this is not always feasible; but this approach can pay dividends and is worth attempting. Keep in mind that no matter how great any idea or advice is, unless YOU choose to implement it and give it a fair shot to work in your life, you're not going to get results.

Let me say that again because it is that important! YOU have to be a part of your own success journey. If you want to see a real, lasting change for the better in your life, you've got to be the biggest part of the process.

So simply knowing that you can offset your negative feelings by introducing positive thoughts into your mind simply isn't enough. No, you've got to actually do it. It's going to mean keeping this inspirational book handy to refer to when you need to. It might mean stopping what you're doing at the moment or even scheduling yourself some time to take in positive or motivational material.

Like dieting or exercising, developing undeniable confidence is a choice. It requires nurturing. It's not always immediate but if you will work on it and cultivate it, you will see results and those around you will as well.

Undeniable Confidence will help you improve and raise your confidence levels to the place where you need them to be.

Throughout this book, you will participate in exciting exercises and assignments, which are more than just learning experiences.

Undeniable Confidence will help you break through all those barriers and fixed notions you have about yourself. Confident people tend to be successful people. They stick it out until they get what they want. This is because they confidently believe in their ability to accomplish their goals.

The lack of confidence can hold you back in achieving the important goals of your life. You cannot impress anyone if you lack confidence. You don't want to be timid and quiet when the world around you is confident and brimming with life, do you? So, fight the coyness and get what you want: SELF-CONFIDENCE! The undeniable kind...

THE POWER OF UNDENIABLE CONFIDENCE

"When your foundation is built on God and you walk in humility, you lose your falsely-assumed attitudes of egotism and self-importance." --- Hasheem Francis

Very often, having undeniable confidence is looked at as the ultimate social skill. We all crave it, and for good reason. People with self-confidence usually find the world a much better place than those who suffer from a lack of it. It is almost as though confident people see the world through rose-tinted glasses.

Why is this? Why do people with self-confidence lead so much better lives? Here are some reasons why confidence is such a highly sought after trait:

Confidence Breeds Trust

People usually find it a lot easier to trust a confident person. Please note, there is a big difference between confidence and over-confidence, the latter of which does not breed trust at all! When you go to a job interview full of confidence in your ability to fulfil the position, the interviewer will take notice. And They will get the feeling that you are capable of performing the tasks required in the job scope.

When you ask someone out on a date, a confident person gives the girl (or guy) the feeling that they are in good hands and they trust that a good time will be had.

A confident person is like someone wearing an invisible sign that reads: "I can do anything, and I can do it well!" The first instinct would be to trust that person.

Confidence Reproduces Affection

Confident people are well liked by their family, their peers, their colleagues, their business associates, their friends and anyone they meet on a personal level, really.

This may be due to the fact that confidence is akin to happiness and people enjoy the company of happy people—this is a fact. After all, would you enjoy the company of a miserable person? No, I didn't think so. A confident person is a happy person, and a happy person always has more friends than a miserable person.

Confidence Commands Authority

When a confident person speaks, people listen. Maybe it's in the way they talk, what they're saying or the reason why they're saying it.

We will never know what exactly the reason is but the reality is that confident people find it so much easier to get other people to cooperate with them.

If confident people can breed trust and happiness in everyone they meet, and can convince people to listen and adhere to what they say, then it only follows that they will have a much easier path in life than most people.

Undeniable confidence is truly a magical thing and the best part is that it's something everyone and anyone can learn and develop.

So if you wish to benefit from the advantages of self-confidence, now would be a good time to start developing your confidence.

The 5 Characteristics of Undeniably Confident People

Do you often look at a person who exudes confidence in everything that they do and think to yourself, "I wish I could be more like that person. I hate being constantly afraid of failure and worrying about what others think of me. How do they do it?"

Well, the good news is that you're not alone. Many other people in the world suffer from a lack of confidence and continue to suffer simply because they believe there's nothing they can do about it.

But this couldn't be further from the truth. Undeniable confidence is something that you can foster and grow within until one day, you will feel like a completely different person with a new lease on life.

So if you, like most of the world, can relate to the above, then here are the **5 characteristics of Undeniably Confident People** that you should start to cultivate within yourself:

1. Undeniably Confident People Believe in Themselves

Confidence comes from within. If you believe in your ability to make the right decisions and choose the right paths, then you are well on your way. This does not mean you should stifle others around you with your beliefs but instead, quietly stand firm on your own ground, trusting your instincts and knowledge you've gained from your life.

2. Undeniably Confident People Learn From Their Mistakes

Contrary to what you may believe, a confident person makes mistakes, too! The only difference is how they deal with their mistakes. Instead of dwelling on their inadequacies and how things could have been done differently, they focus on the future and use the experience as a reminder not to repeat the same blunders.

3. Undeniably Confident People Don't Compare Themselves to Others

This is a big problem for many of us. What we don't realize is that if we continue to compare ourselves to others, there will always be someone who is faster than us, have more money than us, and are better looking than us. The key is in realizing your own strengths and weaknesses, and knowing that other people have their own, too. Instead of wishing you had something that someone else has, it is much more productive to focus on your strengths and get ahead!

4. Undeniably Confident People Believe They Have the Right to be Happy

Undeniably confident people will always go after what they want, regardless of the obstacles that lay ahead or the criticism they may have to endure. This is because they know that they have the right, just like everyone else in the world, to fight for their happiness and to follow whatever path they believe will lead to it.

5. Undeniably Confident People Are Not Stubborn

Although they have great faith in themselves, their abilities and their decisions, they also know when to take advice and when to change course if necessary. They take the time to see things from the other person's point of view instead of simply disregarding it, because they know the importance of having a balanced perspective.

We know the above insight will help you move forward and look at life with more drive, enthusiasm and confidence. The road will not be short or simple, but it will be worth it.

Real Life Examples of Undeniable Confidence

Grace Gordon was a member of a women's empowerment group in her local community. At age 28, she was shy to speak up with friends or in crowds. During a national convention for the women's group, Grace was unexpectedly asked to speak to the members. After the initial panic and fear, she slowly found herself relaxing.

She took several deep breaths and gave herself a pep talk as she walked towards the pulpit. She was finally able to give an anxiety-free talk to the group. Grace was taking a confidence building course at the time and was only two weeks into it. She applied what she learned and in the process, was able to overcome her fears.

Let's take the case of 32-year-old Aaron Goldstein. He was a skilled website designer and though his resume exhibited his credentials, he would never really voice them. Since most jobs required him to interact with clients, Aaron failed to make an impression on prospective employers due to his lack of communication skills and self-confidence. Luckily, Aaron enrolled himself in a confidence building course and applied what he learned. Within a few weeks, he was able to successfully get through an interview without stumbling over his words with an international firm.

Now isn't that a very positive note upon which to begin confidence building? This section is all about self-discovery. Unless you know where you are, how will you move to where you want to be?

Take the assessment below and all will be revealed!

Before we begin confidence building exercises that will work on areas where you need more confidence, take these two assessment tests:

****

Confidence Evaluator
****

Rate the following statements from 0 to 10 based on how much you believe each of them to be true.
- ➢ **0 would mean that you don't believe in the statement at all and that it's utter nonsense.**

- ➢ **10 would mean that you think the statement is completely true.**

****
Statements
****

- ◆ I like myself as a person. _____
- ◆ I am as good as everyone else. _____
- ◆ When I look at myself in the mirror I like what I see. _____
- ◆ I don't feel like an overall failure. _____
- ◆ I am happy to be me. _____
- ◆ I respect myself. _____
- ◆ I'd rather be me than anyone else. _____
- ◆ What others say to me has no affect. _____
- ◆ I enjoy communicating with others. _____
- ◆ I have the skills and qualities to make myself a success. _____
- ◆ I like to take risks. _____
- ◆ I am not afraid to make mistakes. _____
- ◆ I can laugh at myself. _____

Now add up your points for a total score: _____

Do you want to know where your confidence level stands?

If you scored:

100 – 130

You have a high level of self-esteem and confidence. All you have to do is fine tune it and increase your confidence in areas where you'd need it the most.

65 – 99

You have a medium to high ranking in self-esteem. While most of the time you are okay, there are times when you can feel that you need to be motivated. You need more consistent feelings that you are confident and learn to experience these on a regular basis.

30 – 64

You have low levels of self-esteem. You lack confidence in yourself in most areas and need to develop a confidence building plan, and that's why you are reading this book.

0 – 29

You have reached rock bottom and think that everything and everyone is against you. You are stuck in a rut and need to get out of it quickly.

Are you shocked by the results of the Confidence Evaluator? Wait! If you are, there's nothing to hide or feel ashamed about. What are you going to do now in order to build your confidence?

What you could do is write down some of the observations you made while taking this assessment.

What do you specifically need to concentrate on with regards to building up your confidence?

Upon what does a strong sense of self-worth depend: Money? Good looks? High intelligence? Nice clothes? An important job? An expensive car? What if I were to tell you that you can be confident without any of those things?

You don't believe me? Well, it's true! Just as you can smile for no particular reason (simply raise the corner of your mouth) and laugh for no particular reason (try it), you also can be confident without any particular reason. You do not need permission from anybody to be confident.

Many people think confidence has to be based on achievements. Confidence comes from the inside—no one can give it to you, just

as they cannot make you rich, or more handsome or more beautiful. It is all up to YOU! I know you may desire a quick fix to increase your confidence, but developing confidence is a process.
So, where are you now? When you enter a room full of strangers, do you:

A. Sink into a corner and watch?

B. Look for another person who's alone and team up?

C. Stride around the room, greeting everyone as you go?

It does not matter where you are; there is always room for improvement. Confidence is entirely a matter of the mind. It may be a fact that you are not tall, able to wear designer clothes or drive a sports car at this time, but you can still be confident.

It is your attitude that counts; this is not theory. When I first met my wife Deborah over 15 years ago, I was only making $6.15 an hour and didn't have a college degree. She had a Master's degree and a salary-paying job. Deborah never knew how much I made because my attitude was that of a multi-millionaire. When she found out that I did not have a college education, she was in shock but still could not resist this stud. It was the confidence in myself that won her over; I knew I was going to be wealthy in a matter of time.

We are going to share with you our secret weapons for building confidence. The only requirement we have is that you apply them immediately.

Visualization: See yourself as the person you desire to be. Create that vision and live the vision. This exercise took me from $6.15 an hour to millions.

Affirmations: Develop the habit of speaking positive words to yourself. Your voice is the sweetest sound to your ears. Remember, you cannot expect someone else to speak nice things to you if you are not willing to.

Record Yourself: Set aside at least 15 minutes and record yourself either on camera or with an audio recorder. Have a good friend critique you. Also, leave a message on your phone and listen to how you sound when you leave messages on someone else's voicemail. This is to help you become confident with your own image and voice.

Do Not Compare Yourself to Others: Be Authentic. No one respects a "me, too" attitude. Be who God created YOU to be. Find your true self and love it.

5 Fun Ways to Regain Your Confidence
Is the daily grind of monotony getting you down? Are you tired of doing the same old things in the same old pattern at the same old place every day of your life?

If you are living in a regular pattern, doing the same thing day in and day out, you may be asking questions like: "Where am I heading? Is this all there is to life?" And yet, you find yourself unwilling to change, preferring instead to stick to what you know.

Well, the truth is that you may be getting too comfortable in your comfort zone; and unfortunately, this can be extremely detrimental to your feelings of self-worth and self-confidence.

If the above describes you even in just one area, then it's time to break out of the mold and inject some much needed enthusiasm and confidence into your life.

Here are 5 great ways to do just that!

1. Join a Public Speaking Class

Enroll in a drama class or a poetry class. Not only will this give you something new and exciting to do every week, but learning to speak in front of total strangers will boost your confidence and ability to convey messages. This will transfer over to your conduct in the workplace, giving you greater assurance in presenting and elucidating your ideas to your superiors.

2. Take Yourself to New Places

This can be something simple like taking a different road home from work, shopping at a new mall or supermarket, or even going on vacation to somewhere you have never been. Putting yourself in new situations will challenge your perceptions; and not only will you realize new things about your old habits, you will start seeing things from a new point of view.

3. Join a Club

Join a book club, an investment club, toastmasters, or anything of interest to you. The challenge is to be able to meet new people and work with them. You will notice and learn new things about yourself and about the theme of the club you have joined while increasing your business and personal contacts.

4. Learn a New Sport

This is a great one! By the time you hit 30, many people stop learning new sports and often stop playing the old ones, too! But there is nothing like exercise and sports to build confidence, and teamwork to foster camaraderie. In addition, learning something that you never thought you would learn will go a long way towards building the "I can do anything!" mentality that is so important in life.

5. Volunteer at a Charity

There are tons of charities in almost every city. Pick one and volunteer once a week. The joy and appreciation you will see on the faces of the people you meet will literally be 'Chicken Soup for your Soul!' And spending time with those less fortunate or with those reaching the twilight of their lives will make you take a closer look at your own life and learn to be grateful for what you have. Maybe it's time you started living more of your life before it is too late!

Ultimately, the best way to get out of a rut is to start being more spontaneous. Start doing new things, different things. Accept invitations where before you may have rejected them.

Living a life full of vibrancy and spontaneity is the best present you can give to yourself. You will be a more assertive, confident and happier person.

CONDITIONING YOUR BELIEFS

"Applied faith is stronger than fear, so why focus on the weaker?" --- Deborah Francis

Have you completed the Confidence Evaluator?

What was your score?

What you can do now is write down two things you would love to develop with regards to your confidence.

1.

2.

The secret of success lies in a visual image of how you would want to act, walk, talk, think and move your body so that you know what to aspire for. Although you would like to believe that some people are born with undeniable confidence, most of them learn or acquire it as they grow from experience.

Confidence is everything because you will be proud of who you are, what you do and what you say. People will also trust and have faith in you if you have confidence in yourself. If you don't believe in yourself, no one else will.

If you lack confidence, you will find it difficult or even impossible to take leadership roles. The most successful men and women build undeniable confidence in themselves and in whatever they do.

Undeniable confidence will also help you overcome challenges in life. It will help you make decisions quickly and a put off any doubts which you may have on the probability of the success, or failure, of the task you want to undertake. Research has shown that most people are reluctant to back or approve something which was proposed by someone who at the time of leadership was fumbling, apologetic or nervous.

You will persuade most people if you hold your head high, answer questions directly with confidence and openly admit when you do not know something. Gaining the confidence of others is always termed as success and you should aim at doing so all the time. As stated earlier, undeniable confidence can be learned or acquired if you are willing to put in the necessary work to develop it.

Remember, the goal is to develop *Undeniable Confidence*! ☺

Your Past and Present is the Key to Your Future

Knowing more about who you are will give you the insight for your future goals. Where are you going?

This isn't about location—it's about focus and achievement in your life. Pretty big stuff, but not so big that you can't get your hands around it and get down to the basics so you can achieve your goals.

Did you accomplish what you set out to do last month? Or did you even have an idea of what you wanted to accomplish?

If not, did you play the blame game? Was it the economy again? Or the competition you face? Or did your boss change the rules again?

If you have read anything about goals, principled leadership or even goal-setting from an achievement perspective, you realize that every one of us allows something to get in the way. It's part of that negative, skeptical thought pattern engrained inside of us. You just naturally create barriers. But there is good news: Barriers are meant to be jumped over! Don't despair. I like to think about how Thomas Edison often referred to the 10,000 possibilities that failed to make an electric light bulb. Failure is only the teacher for success. When you find those golden nuggets disguised in what look like a failed situation, then you can move on to success. You can learn more in the valley than you can on the mountain top.

One way to do that is to focus on your past and your present, and use it to inform your future. First, we'll look at your past—all of those great, terrible, wonderful, unique experiences in your life that make you who you are. If you look back in your past, I'll bet you remember those pivotal experiences that were surprises and not expected, as well as those experiences you wanted to happen and then found them not as rewarding as you had anticipated.

Disappointment is also an important confidence teacher like success and self-awareness. Any time you find out what gives you a sense of value, that experience is worth whatever it costs you.

Regarding your present: Is it what you expected? Are you happy, fulfilled and motivated? Or are you blaming someone else for the failures in your life? Many of us are not even aware what causes these feelings.

The point is, never stop looking, asking questions, reading and studying. If you stop being curious about what was going on around you when you left high school or college, then you have missed most of what living is all about. Those two venues were only there to prepare you for a lifetime of discovery and adventure. Success requires lots of diligent thinking, hard work and perseverance. If someone told you it would be easy, then they told you a lie. If they told you it would be the greatest thing you ever experienced, then they told you the truth.

Your future is a jar full of dreams, possibilities and glory. It is the substance that drives someone to achieve anything. Success is born out of a lot of practice, study and focused effort over many years.

These all program our minds to recognize those moments of serendipity and discovery. All of this means having a central point of principle which drives us to measure all our actions in light of our central desires. It often means taking risks.

If you are saying at this point, "You just don't understand my situation. It just isn't possible right now to...," then you are afraid to risk what you have now in order to get what you really want in the future. You think it's more important to hold onto what you have now than to reach for a lifetime dream. You haven't really assessed what you really have and what you can give up. You haven't determined what your principles are and how you are going to change your own actions to realize that dream.

Combine the past, present and future into the image of what you want to become. Your mind was wonderfully made to allow you to grow into who you want to become. The sad fact is many of us grew into what someone else told us to be and never listened to that still voice inside that said; Be and do YOU!

Now it's up to you. Educate yourself about your interests and perform at your best—every time. Develop an inner discipline and find the central principles that drive you.

PRACTICAL
There must be someone in your life who has high self-esteem and whose confidence levels you admire: a colleague, friend, family member or even a famous personality who oozes self-confidence.

This is your chance to start from scratch to improve the way you walk, talk and think, including your body language.

In the following exercise, you are going to describe why the person you admire is really worth that admiration.

MY CONFIDENCE ROLE MODEL
He/she would act like…

He/she would talk like…

He/she would walk like…

He/she would think like…

Their body language would be like…

Other people think that this person is…

When faced with problems, this person…

Now take note of the few things you have written down. This exercise is not to imitate someone else but to get a clear picture in your mind of what a confident person looks like in your eyes. The purpose is to make an effort to be like YOU. Put those same qualities into action. Yes! You heard it right:

ACT AS IF YOU ARE THE PERSON YOU WANT TO BECOME, AND NOTICE THE RESULTS!

Don't worry if this feels awkward, because it will! It will take a while for it to sink in and feel normal.

You will also need a strong inner belief system to be the confident person you want to become. Self-acceptance gives you the much needed energy and room to grow. Your inner belief system helps

---

you develop an ability to accept yourself: who you are, and what you feel, think and do.

The benefits of a strong inner belief system are varied and great:

- ♦ Stronger self-confidence
- ♦ Healthy self-esteem
- ♦ Greater life satisfaction
- ♦ Comfort with self and others

But how is this inner belief system developed?

Consider the following questions. Finding the answers can help you to weed out the muck of what "everybody else says" and get back to the purity and perfection of self-expression.

1. What are your current beliefs about work, life, people and yourself?

_____
_____
_____
_____
_____
_____
_____
_____
_____

2. How much of what you believe is your own original ideology? _____

_____
_____
_____
_____

* Take a look at what you wrote on each page.

* What messages may have come from parents, friends, family, peers, teachers, etc.?

* Now, pick out and highlight the things you feel truly reflect who you are and what you believe.

3. Are the messages that came from others empowering or limiting? _____

_____

_____

_____

_____

_____

_____

4. Now, look at the messages that reflect your own inner belief system. Are those empowering or limiting? _____

_____

_____

_____

_____

_____

5. How do they make you feel? _____

_____

_____

_____

_____

_____

_____

6. What do you <u>want</u> to believe? _____

_____

_____

_____

_____

_____

_____

_____

_____

* Does these beliefs reflect how you want to feel about life, work, people and yourself?

* Write down each idea or thought on the left-hand side of a page and on the right-hand side, write how you would like to feel or think about each idea.

*Reprogram yourself by identifying these limiting thoughts as they pop into your head and replacing them with the thoughts and ideas that empower you.

* If you continue this exercise, you will find the old limiting thoughts creeping up less and less, and new empowering thoughts will begin to take their place.

7. What messages about life, people, work and yourself did you get from family as you shaped your personality? _____

_____

_____

_____

_____

_____

_____

* Messages from family members are repetitive and will keep coming up.

* If you have chosen to reprogram any of their thoughts, values and beliefs, then be prepared to defend yourself and counter these beliefs whenever a family member articulates them.

8. What is your response when you express your belief and someone disagrees? _____

_____
_____
_____
_____
_____
_____
_____

* How should you respond when you share your beliefs with others and find that they disagree?

* Here is a hint: do not change your mind. It is okay that someone else believes differently from you—that is what makes the world go round.

* Simply state that you see life, work, people, etc. differently, and then repeat and reconfirm your belief to yourself.

These questions, their answers and the exercises associated with each are sure to strengthen your belief system. The challenge is to develop confidence in your ability to express these beliefs in an unwavering fashion.

There will always be people who will disregard your beliefs. What you have to do is test your ability to continue with your belief system and keep it intact as part of your personal growth.

Take the reigns of your life into your hands. Refrain from talking to a lot of people concerning this new concept of undeniable confidence until you have a firm grip on it yourself and feel secure about explaining what you have learned to others. Remember, hearing negative comments from people who do not understand the truth will not do you any good, and it may only cause you self-doubt. *If you buy someone else's opinion, then you buy their lifestyle.*

Moving ahead in the process, once your belief system has been strengthened, you will find that people who have less confidence in their own beliefs will seek you out.

You can now help and encourage others and tap them into your own belief system, following the process you used to get where you are now.

Well, what are you waiting for?

Start now!

CHECK THOSE NEGATIVE THOUGHTS

"Your own aspirations influence the aspirations of others. Accepting yourself not only as you are but as you can become—the better you - is your great enterprise." --- **Hasheem Francis**

Achieving a level of personal confidence that was previously unknown is much closer than you think. But first, it's important to stay in touch with the present. "Stay in touch with the present? I'm thinking… I'm already IN the present!"

Well, certainly we all are in the present since there is nowhere else to be, but that doesn't mean our thoughts are in the present—and therein lie the challenges to our confidence. We as humans are the rarest of all species in that not only can we think, but we can think about our thinking.

You can use this process of being aware of your self-thoughts to help you achieve confidence. It is important for you to challenge what you see and believe. This insures that your view of the world matches reality. So often, what we believe is the truth is nothing more than glimpses of the past, present and future.

We often take only the bad from the past, quickly breeze through the present and falsely make up the future. The result is frequently guilt about your imperfect past, anxiety about a future that doesn't exist and impatience with the "Now."

But it is the Now which can help us to live our lives today, fully alive, happy and with confidence. Rarely do we allow ourselves the opportunity to enjoy the moment. But the moment is the only reality we know. It is exactly the way it should be and it cannot be anything more than that.

But we repeatedly make it out to be different. And by doing so, we have lost the opportunity to fully experience the rain, children playing, the learning to be achieved by listening to the world seen through a grandparent's eyes, or a friend sharing one of his or her own moments. Many times, we are too caught up in what will happen, or what has happened, to experience what IS happening.

This is not to say that planning for the future is unimportant or that reminiscing is not useful and enjoyable. But unfortunately, too often, we become entangled in a fictitious future and stifled by our predictions.

We run from the saber-toothed tiger that no longer exists in our modern-day world. That tiger has been replaced with confronting a friend, giving a speech, driving over a bridge or feeling discomfort from changing a habit.

We create absolute horror from an uncertain future that we make real in the present; but staying in the moment awards you the opportunity to see the world as it is, not as you believe it should or could be. It allows you to observe the truth and look at real data, not information couched in fears and anxiety.

And it is this truth which will allow you to enjoy yourself, others and the world around you because it is exactly as it should be. You can manage any life event that presents itself. You can choose to do it with or without confidence.

Even the most positive person has negative thoughts!

Olympian John Konrads won one gold and one bronze medal in the 1960 Rome Olympics. During the 400-meter freestyle, for which Konrads won the bronze medal, he said he lost focus by nurturing negative thoughts on how arch-rival Murray was going to perform.

Konrads confessed that though he had convinced himself he could win, the thoughts of doubt got in the way and hindered his chances.

Actually, negative thoughts are commonplace and anyone can be a 'victim' to them. However, it is not the presence of negative thoughts but the way we handle and react to them that either breaks or makes our confidence and self-esteem.

Think about this:

NOTHING HAS ANY MEANING IN LIFE, ONLY THE MEANING YOU GIVE TO IT.

If you ALLOW negative thoughts to HARM you, THEY WILL!

If you ALLOW negative thoughts to HELP you, THEY WILL!

Before we get into this section, it is important to keep a few points in mind:
- You are not the only one who has negative thoughts; everyone on this planet has them.
- You are not making an attempt to uproot negative thoughts, just handling them more intelligently.
- Negative thoughts, as such, do not harm you. It's what you say to yourself after the thought has entered your mind that harms you.
- You can change any thought you want by changing what it means to you.

Analyzing your Thoughts

Want to increase your confidence? You have to first find out what triggers those negative thoughts and emotions you have about yourself. It becomes easier to analyze and respond to them if you write them down.

FYI, it is not the trigger or the event that instigates the bad feelings. What makes you feel despondent are the internal dialogues you say to yourself in response to the trigger.

These catalysts distort reality and put your feelings in turmoil.

That is the kind of turmoil Joann got into. Her husband Roger had been quite distracted over the past few days. Joann tried talking to him on a couple of occasions but he was not forthcoming. She heard him talking in hushed tones over the phone, and he also came home late more often. Joann was perturbed beyond words. She spent hours talking to herself, wondering what Roger was up to.

She would have thought:
+ **"He's ignoring me."**
+ **"Maybe he's having an affair with someone."**
+ **"He doesn't find me attractive or interesting anymore."**

She would have felt:
+ **Anger**
+ **Resentment**
+ **Grief**
+ **Self-pity**

Maybe she could have been more probing or given more time to her husband. Did she know her husband well enough to arrive at these conclusions? Roger could have been having a tough time at work—a bad review by the boss, a fall in profits in business or tiff with a colleague. It could have been anything! Roger could have had a completely unrelated problem but to Joann, it looked like a problem in their relationship!

Controlling your inner voice and what you say to yourself either makes or breaks your self-esteem and confidence. Within this section, you will be introduced to a technique that you can use to control your inner dialogue and to make you appraise just how hard and unreasonable you are on yourself. But before we get into the exercise, let's discuss those negative thoughts you have.

Here is a little recap: *It is not the trigger or the event that instigates the bad feelings but the internal dialogues you say to yourself in response to the trigger that makes you despondent.*

Okay, to make it easier to understand, let's split these negative thoughts or distortions into 13 categories.

Here's the list you can use as a quick reference:

1. **Assuming**
2. **Over-generalizing**
3. **Should's**
4. **Labeling**
5. **Binning the positives**
6. **And they all lived happily ever after**
7. **Blaming other people and events**
8. **It's all or nothing**
9. **Negative thinking erodes your soul**
10. **Believing what you feel**
11. **Personalizing**
12. **Making comparisons with others**
13. **I can't cope with life**

While we go through each of them, make notes of the ones you use most frequently.

1. Assuming

When you make assumptions about things without having facts, you are assuming the worst without knowing the full picture or testing the evidence.

Let's go back to our example about Joann and her husband. She did not have any of the facts; she just assumed that her relationship with her husband was in deep trouble. She could have tested the assumption by asking, "Roger, did I do something that upset you? What is wrong? I think we should talk this out."

2. Over-generalizing

This is when you over-generalize your thoughts and make them more intense by the words you use.

For instance, you would say things like:
- **"I always end up on the losing side."**
- **"I make mistakes in everything I do."**
- **"Everyone hates me."**
- **"Everyone thinks I am so dumb."**

Even when you read these lines, their demoralizing effect is so evident! Although you know that such over-generalizing internal dialogues are inaccurate, unjust, unfair and affect your confidence, you still use them.

How do you turn this around?

Well, a better phrase to use would be, "I'm willing to take on this project, and I will give it my all." Look for the good in every situation and what works well. It can do wonders!

3. Should's

Some people surround themselves with "Should's."

- **"I should be thinner."**
- **"I should have more friends."**
- **"I should be earning more money."**

Are you the kind of person who says "should" all the time?

These are the demands you place on yourself. They represent what you are not doing but you think you should be!

So when you know you should be doing something but are not doing it, how do you feel?

Inadequate, hopeless, frustrated? Yes, the list can go on and on.

So, what are your plans to get rid of the "should's?" _____

_____

_____

_____

_____

_____

_____

_____

_____

It's easy: Just change the "should" to "want" or "could."

- **"I want to do this."**
- **"I could do this!"**

4. Labeling

How often do you use an adjective to describe yourself? Labeling is a common syndrome. This is when you give yourself a name or statement that describes who you are.

For example:
- ♦ **"I am a loser."**
- ♦ **"I am stupid."**
- ♦ **"I am ugly."**
- ♦ **"I am fat."**

How is it possible that you are a loser in every aspect of your life? Is there nothing in you that is attractive? Of course not!

Stop labeling yourself and be specific in your thoughts.

Instead of saying, "I am a loser because my boss did not like how I completed the project," say, "That didn't work out the way I would have liked, but it was a learning experience."

5. Binning the positives

Do you tend to overlook the compliments people give you? Do you refuse to accept, or simply ignore, if someone says: "That was a great job; well done" or "You look fantastic today"?

Do you usually reply to praise by saying: "Oh, it was nothing; it was easy" or "I really don't look great; you're just saying that"?

Do you realize that you have just discounted the fact that you worked really hard to get that project done, or you take time to get your appearance right?

Let's set the record straight: A simple "Thank you" with a smile is the perfect response.

Think it over. Is it that much of an effort?

You would give credit to someone who did a great job. Make sure you accept the credit when you do a great job or when you receive a compliment.

6. And they all lived happily ever after

Perfection is an illusion. Oh, yes, it is. No point arguing there.

So if you are a person who has to have everything perfect in your life, it's going to be a pretty tough road! You are setting yourself up for disappointments.

Do you have thoughts like:
- **"That shouldn't happen to me."**
- **"I can't believe that just happened."**
- **"That's so unfair."**

Stop looking for that perfect world. Everyone has things happen to them, good and bad. You are not a special case and no one is exempt. Accept that we all go through trials and ask yourself: "What could I do to improve this situation right now?" or "What can I learn from this?"

7. Blaming other people and events

Do you blame others and not accept responsibility for outcomes that are different from your expectations?

Do you say:
- **"If only my parents had more money, I would have been successful by now."**
- **"If they accepted my ideas, we would be so much further along."**
- **"He makes me feel so unloved."**
- **"She had a hold over me, which means I can't do anything."**

While this attitude is unfruitful, it will also make you feel like a victim. With this mentality, you will move ahead with a sense of helplessness, thinking that you are not capable of anything successful.

The events you experience in life can have an effect on you but at the end of the day, only you have the control on how you will respond to these events.

So, how do you turn these thoughts around?

Well, for starters, focus on the reality. If you feel something is unfair or unjust, accept that it is.

Then accept that the impact it has on you is your responsibility.

8. It's all or nothing

There's more than just black and white—there are several colors in between, right? Like blue, green, red, yellow, pink, brown, purple, mauve... phew! Are you one of those people who think that it's all or nothing?

Is there no gray area in between?
- **"I'm either a success or a failure."**
- **"If I get first place, I'm a winner. If I get second place, I'm a loser (irrespective of the other 5,000 runners)!"**
- **"If I don't get things 100% perfect, I'm a flop."**
- **"If I don't make a million dollars in business, then my business is a failure."**

In life, there are rarely successes and failures—success is a journey, not a destination.

Successes and failures are not meant to be measured on a 0 to 100 scale. At the end of the day if you don't perform to your highest standards, it certainly doesn't mean you scored 0!

Your all or nothing thinking is only setting you up for failure. How many times do you perform with absolute perfection?

Less than 10% of the time! So, does that mean you are a failure 90% of the time? Now you know that is utter nonsense.

9. Negative thinking erodes your soul

How do you react to events that don't work out the way you planned? For instance, if your boss comes into your office and says that you completed a project incorrectly, do you react negatively and let it affect the rest of your day?

Your thoughts can make the entire situation negative, but what happens if you change your focus when you start thinking negatively?

You can say:
- **"What is still good about this situation?"**
- **"That is only one bad report. What can I learn from this?"**
- **"What could I still enjoy about this experience?"**

10. Believing what you feel

Feelings are not facts! If you blindly believe your feelings, you may suffer undue disappointment. Mend your ways or you are sure to suffer a confidence setback.

So, are you the type of person who believes all the feelings you have?
- **"I feel bad; therefore, I must be bad."**
- **"I feel like a loser; therefore, I must be a loser."**
- **"I feel ugly; therefore, I must be ugly."**

Low levels of confidence can distort your thoughts. So you really need to make sure your feelings do not paint a false picture.

Ask yourself questions like:
- ◆ **"What would someone who is a loser look like?"**
- ◆ **"Am I really like that?"**

Challenge your feelings by questioning them. If you desire to change or improve your results in your life, you must change your thoughts immediately. You are "Built To Prosper" and your confidence is contained in your thoughts. So be good to yourself, choose magnificent ideas and stop permitting your physical world to control your thinking.

11. Personalizing

Personalizing is when you blame yourself for things that are out of your control.

It happens when you say:
- ◆ **"It is entirely my fault that my department didn't get a pay increase this year."**
- ◆ **"It is all my fault that our department got downsized."**

Blaming yourself for others' actions and decisions means that you are taking too much responsibility on your shoulders. Don't do it! You are not accountable for someone else's actions or decision-making.

12. Making comparisons with others

Do you always compare yourself to others? If you do, it's time to stop. Why are you putting yourself through worthless, unhealthy competition?

What you're doing when you compare yourself to others is magnifying your weaknesses and others' strengths, or shrinking others' weaknesses and your strengths.

So, are you saying something like this?

- ♦ **"I don't have a chance at landing that vice president position; who would promote a person without a college degree? Janet is young and has her MBA."**
- ♦ **"I am hopeless at getting others to follow my ideas. Chad is great at that; he can get others to follow him with no problem at all."**

Challenge these thoughts! If you don't lift yourself up, don't expect someone else to do it. Appreciate that you are a unique person and stop these distortions.

13. I can't cope with life

If you find yourself saying things like:

- ♦ **"I can't stand it."**
- ♦ **"I couldn't live without you."**
- ♦ **"I can't manage this."**

When you are making these statements, you are accepting defeat and telling yourself that you are not strong enough to cope with life. Yes, a lot of circumstances in life can be unpleasant and challenging. **But you can overcome any difficult situation!**

A better way of thinking is:

- ♦ **"I don't really like this, but it won't stop me from accomplishing my goals. There is something I can learn from this to use to my advantage."**
- ♦ **"If this does happen, will I really be helpless and unable to cope? Absolutely not!"**
- ♦ **"When I look back 20 years from now, will anyone really care about this?"**

Building Confidence from Setbacks

One of the strangest things to me about the human psyche is that almost everyone is afraid of failure.

Most people are afraid of being laughed at, looked down upon, falling flat on their face or having someone call them a loser. This, to an extent, is understandable because none of these are particularly nice things.

But the real fact of the matter is that with the right attitude, failure can be your best friend. In fact, if you ask any successful person, they would unequivocally tell you that you cannot achieve success without tasting some form of failure along the way. How you handle that failure will ultimately shape your destiny.

Follow these insights to get the most out of your failure and come out from your low points with more undeniable confidence than ever before:

Learn more from your mistakes

Embrace your errors because without them, you cannot grow. Getting something right is great, but you don't learn anything other than what you already know is true. But making a mistake means that you now have the opportunity to learn something new and get it right the second time. Failures allow us to improve ourselves, which is essentially what life is about—a journey of self-improvement.

Never make the same mistake twice
Every time you get something wrong, or fail in doing something, you need to ask yourself, "What can I learn from this so I never make this same mistake again?" Without truly understanding the reasons for your failure, you can neither grow nor ensure that the mistake does not repeat itself.

Don't play the blame game

Many people tend to throw blame onto others by saying, "It was his fault for messing it up," or "Everything could have gone smoothly if it was not for her." Playing the blame game gets you nowhere. Focus instead on what could be done to alleviate such problems from resurfacing.

There's nowhere to go but up

One of the best things about failing is that it usually cannot get any worse. And as long as you keep trying, you are bound to eventually succeed, and then all your failures will be nothing but the memories of the past.

With these concepts in mind, you stand to gain more confidence from your mistakes. And as the eternal saying goes, *"What does not kill you can only make you stronger!"*

UNLEASH THE GENIUS IN YOU

"The eyes are the window of the soul. Study the eyes of successful men and women and you will find that everyone possesses intensity of purpose." --- **Deborah Francis**

Sometimes it can be really difficult finding the positive side in the challenges confronting us. When dealing with adversity, a career setback, the ending of a long-time relationship or the illness of a child, it's hard to believe there is a sunny side or a silver lining to the experience. But history is full of people who found possibilities through adversity, and reflecting on their achievements can remind us to look for opportunities in dark times:

If a young Spanish soccer star had not been injured seriously in a car accident and spent months recuperating in the hospital, he likely would not have discovered his musical side. The world might have missed the beautiful voice of Julio Iglesias.

McDonald's with its golden arches would not exist today if Ray Kroc had succeeded in his first several business ventures. Instead, they ended in bankruptcy prior to his opportune meeting with the McDonald brothers when he purchased a little hamburger stand which later become the world's preeminent fast-food franchise.

Had Walt Disney not failed in his initial dreams to the point of bankruptcy, the magic of the Magic Kingdom and the hundreds of Disney-related businesses would not exist today.

"Every adversity, every failure, and every heartache carries with it the seed of an equivalent or greater benefit." --- **Napoleon Hill**

It is tough to understand, but sometimes we are taught lessons in adversity that will benefit us. Allow yourself to be open to what life is teaching you and apply it later when the opportunity presents itself.

Many challenges are not insurmountable to begin with, they only need a little creativity or fortitude and a gentle nudge from your creative side.

Allowing yourself to have a positive and affirming outlook sometimes seems contrary to what is expected of us. We are taught to belittle ourselves to seem normal so we don't appear prideful. Modesty gets in the way and we are expected to play down our strengths and play up our weaknesses just to help us fit in.

Maintain the attitude and mindset of a creative problem-solver. Learn to develop opportunity awareness. Think about possible benefits hidden even in adversity or hardship. Learn to visualize any negative situation as a chance for metamorphosis like a caterpillar changing into a butterfly. Sometimes creativity calls for looking at a combination of things that you had not thought of previously.

You can learn from people like Ray Croc, Walt Disney and Julio Iglesias and what they had to overcome to reach the pinnacle of success. You must allow yourself to find opportunity in the midst of challenges or tragedy.

Hindrances to Unleashing Your Genius

Media Conditioning: Advertisements are hunting for your commitment so that they can generate revenues from you. As a result, they are trying all sorts of ways to convince you and target your desires and weaknesses. For example, the alcohol ads often portray the ability to attract women but in reality, this is not the case and fantasy is shown much larger than the truth.

Social Conditioning: The people around you, including your family, relatives, friends or superiors, may stop you from seeing the genius within. This may cue to their ability to impart the wrong values into your life.

False Beliefs: False beliefs may hinder you from being truthful. Some husbands use the excuse of being stressful at work to be unfaithful to their wives. How can they possibly justify they are not doing anything wrong?

Emotional Interference: When you have strong emotions, they will usually corrupt your ability to perceive reality. Fear, anger, guilt, shame and frustrations are some of the examples.

Addictions: This is probably one of the hardest to overcome, especially if you have been addicted for a while. Do smokers know that smoking an extra pack of cigarettes is doing them no good? Of course they do! Then why are they still smoking? It is their addiction that stops them from facing the truth.

Immaturity: When you choose not to grow up and you ignore your responsibilities in life, you become known as someone who is not ready to take a leadership role. We all have areas in our life where we can grow. But when you refuse to grow up that is immaturity. Mature people know that they always have room for improvement.

How to Develop the Genius Within

Self-Assessment: You need to sit down and assess different areas of your life. For example, how do you rate your health and fitness? What about mental development and habits? Is your business making money? How well do you handle your emotions? Rank each of them from 1 to 10 with 1 being the weakest and 10 the strongest.

Journaling: Writing in a journal can be very powerful. As you write down your feelings, emotions and thoughts on your personal development process, you will see the truth more clearly. Your journal can be used as a blueprint to remind you of how you got from point A to point B. If you succeeded in the past, you can do it again.

Media Fasting: This can be difficult but amazingly powerful! Remember the times when you kept procrastinating about starting your big project simply because you were on the Internet or watching TV? You wanted to watch another hour of your favorite show or spend another 10 minutes on Facebook or Twitter. If you can make it a habit to fast (take a break) from media, you will be amazed with the results and how much you will get accomplished. It will be much easier to tap into your creative genius and build your confidence.

No one can make you feel inferior without your consent.

It's not what people say to you that affects your confidence; it's what you say to yourself after they've stopped talking that either makes or breaks your self-esteem.

Here are a few feelings and thoughts that you are sure to face at some point, and note what kind of action you can practice in each case:

FEELING: "I don't feel confident about the way I look."
ACTION: Improve your overall appearance. Would losing or putting on (in case you are painfully thin) some weight make you feel great? If so, DO IT! What clothes would your Confidence Role Model wear to feel good? Get a new haircut and treat yourself to some new clothes—it makes you feel better and more confident.

FEELING: "I'm afraid of that person—I'm never confident around them."

ACTION: Just remember that they eat, sleep and go to the bathroom just like you do and mostly have the same problems as you—they just don't show it! How would your Confidence Role Model deal with this person? What would they do? Think of the things you can do that they cannot do. How would they feel if the roles were reversed?

FEELING: "I'm afraid of the feedback and reaction I'm going to get when I complete this project."

ACTION: As long as you have done everything to the best of your ability, you don't have to worry. And if you do make a mistake or two, so what! A person who never makes mistakes is probably not doing anything at all. There are no real failures in life as long as you learn from the outcomes. You are a winner!

FEELING: "I'm really worried about this."

ACTION: Time to usher in your Confidence Role Model and consider: Would they worry about this? How would they deal with this situation? What would they do? In the grand scheme of things, what will worrying do to solve this problem? Is there any action I can take to fix this right now?

FEELING: "My friends are really negative thinkers and this just irritates me when I'm with them."

ACTION: Do not get rid of your friends, unless they are detrimental to your growth. Make sure you surround yourself with positive and progressive people. Surround yourself with people who empower you and challenge you to be more and do more.

FEELING: "I can't do this."

ACTION: Oh, yes, you can! Break the problem down into small chunks and attack each piece separately. Nothing is ever as daunting as it first seems. How would someone that you admire handle this? Think of a time when you completed something really difficult—play it over and over in your mind like a video recording before you do the task at hand.

FEELING: "I never have enough money to do the things that I want."
ACTION: Do you have "more month left at the end of the money" rather than "more money left at the end of the month"? Do you plan your budget? Do you know where all of your money goes? If you answered yes to the first question and no to the next two, it is time you made a plan of action. You may need new career to achieve the lifestyle you want.

FEELING: "I don't feel valuable as a person."
ACTION: Write down your strengths on a piece of paper. Don't forget to list all your achievements in life from your school exams to when you passed your driving test to the job interviews you completed or when you were brave enough to ask that special person out on a date. Remind yourself that you are already successful and you don't have to feel sorry for yourself. After all, no matter where you are in life, there is always someone who is worse off than you.

More Actions

We are not done yet! Write down all of those confidence-destroying statements that you say to yourself or others say to you.

_____
_____
_____
_____
_____
_____
_____

Now, write down what you are going to replace those thoughts with after the statements are made. _____

_____

_____

_____

_____

_____

Confidence-shaping friends and colleagues

The people who you hang out with, family, friends or colleagues, will either have a positive or negative affect on your levels of self-esteem and confidence. You have been around people who are positive, happy and pleasant—they are the ones who make you feel like a welcome sight any day, who smile sincerely and who encourage you rather than rain down on you with advice and reprieves.

Their personality rubs off on you, too, making you feel good about yourself. Such lively people can easily sprinkle zest into a boring atmosphere and fill a room with constructive energy and upbeat vibes.

You must be familiar with the moaners, too.

They're always putting people down, they don't like others being successful, they're jealous and they're negative thinkers. Phew! That's a long list and it can definitely go on and on.

Such people bring down your energy levels in a way that takes you a million miles away from the position at which you really want to be operating. They try and urge you to join their team—a team of non-achievers.

Family members can also be grumblers at times. You can always choose your friends; you can never choose your family!

So what should you do to make sure that the people you hang out with empower and support what you stand for rather than bringing you down all of the time?

1. You have the power to choose who you connect with. Ideally, you want to connect with people who are happy, vibrant and positive. People who are where you want to be and less like those who rain on your parade.

2. If you have good friends who are negative and yet you want to hang around them, make a point of letting them know how you feel—if they are true friends, they will respect you for this. If they are negative from time to time, just acknowledge that this is what they are like and block out the negativity.

3. The same can be applied to family. Your more mature family members have behaviours that have been conditioned for years. Appreciate where they have come from and as stated before, select and elicit the information that filters through to your brain.

BUILDING UNDENIABLE CONFIDENCE

"When you know yourself, you have self-confidence, you know where you are going and how to get there; the determination to succeed shows in your eyes, your speech and in your actions." --- **Hasheem Francis**

Undeniable confidence is essential. You have to discover what works for your own life.

Different people have different methods to building confidence. The most important thing you must do is focus on what works for you, not compete with other people to see if you are more confident than them.

The Power of the Mind is Truly Remarkable

Here are some components of building confidence:

Perception: How you perceive something will affect how you react to it. If you perceive that you need to develop the confidence to be able to speak in front of large crowds, then you will plan ways that will give you the opportunity to speak to more people, and you will develop yourself to the point where you will not fear criticism.

Accuracy: Although clarity is important in decision-making, there is really no such thing as total accuracy. You will never know if the career you choose will turn out to be the best. You will never be guaranteed a successful marriage when you step into a relationship. The best way is still to accept mistakes and minimize risks.

Acceptance: You need to accept the truths of your current situation, no matter how good or bad it is. Accept that your company is not where it needs to be. Accept that your spouse is the best wife you can ever have.

Self-Awareness: Learn more about yourself by being aware of different areas of your life. This includes your strengths, weaknesses, habits, knowledge, desires, emotions and mindsets.

How you feel at any given moment is linked to:
- **What you are focusing on**
- **The way you are moving and using your body**
- **The language you are using**

No doubt, your mind controls all three.

The moment you feel lethargic or need an instant confidence/ energy boost, just change the way you feel by changing these three points:

1. What you are focusing on

Stay conscious of what you are focusing on in any particular moment. What would you have to focus on to feel vibrant and full of energy? What should you focus on to feel confident? On the other hand, if you are feeling vibrant and energized right now, what are you thinking about?

2. The way you are moving and using your body

This is also called your physiology. Emotion is created by motion and the fewer movements you make, the less energy you will have!

Moreover, the type of movements you make either pump you up or make you languid and want to doze off. Observe your body when you are feeling low in confidence.

Are you sitting down? Is your head up or down? Are your shoulders slouched? Are you walking slowly or quickly? Are your facial muscles moving? What are you doing with your hands?

Write down below all the characteristics of a confident person. Imagine there is a confident person before you now. How would they be moving their body?

It's your turn to feel energized and confident. Ready? Okay!

Copy the movements that you just wrote down and work at it until you feel you are in a confident state. If it takes all day, DO IT!

3. The language you are using

The words you say to yourself both in your mind and out aloud will have an impact on how you are feeling. Do you say:

"I'm feeling tired"?
"I'm not smart enough"?
"I'm angry"?
"I'm livid"?
"I'm overwhelmed"?
"I'm depressed"?

Write down some more common phrases that you use, then put an X through them to "delete" or release those emotions.

_____

_____

_____

_____

_____

_____

_____

The intensity of those negative sayings will have an effect on how you feel and whether you feel confident or not.

What if instead of saying, **"I'm really nervous,"** you said to yourself, **"I'm really excited"**?

Would it make you feel better? Of course it would.

The feelings and emotions linked to nervousness and excitement are actually the same, it's just that you're giving the adrenaline right direction. So, what other words could you use to replace the negative sayings?

Try swapping:
"I'm feeling tired" to **"I'm feeling resourceful"**
"I'm stupid" to **"I'm learning"**
"I'm angry" to **"I'm a little annoyed"**
"I'm livid" to **"I'm a little miffed"**
"I'm overwhelmed" to **"I'm feeling busy"**
"I'm feeling insecure" to **"I'm questioning"**
"I'm depressed" to **"I'm not on top of things"**

As the intensity of the words lower, the intensity of the feelings lessen as well.

Let's move on with some simple exercises.

Write down five negative sayings or phrases that you say on a consistent basis and replace them with empowering and less intensified ones:

OLD NEGATIVE PHRASES

1.

2.

3.

4.

5.

NEW EMPOWERING PHRASES

1.

2.

3.

4.

5.

Just as you lower the intensity of words to lessen negative feelings, you can apply the reverse to feel magnificent and confident every single day! Change your vocabulary to improve the quality of your day.

Instead of saying **"I feel good,"** say **"I feel fantastic!"** It's as simple as that.

Here are some more examples. Change:
"I feel ok" to **"I feel awesome"**
"I feel motivated" to **"I am driven"**
"I feel confident" to **"I feel unstoppable"**
"I feel energized" to **"I feel juiced"**

Change the "good" words of the present to "magnificent" words of the future. When you implement this, the impact will be AWESOME!

OLD "GOOD" PHRASES

1.

2.

3.

4.

5.

NEW "MAGNIFICENT" PHRASES

1.

2.

3.

4.

5.

HOW TO LEAD WITH CONFIDENCE

"What I think of myself is predicated on who I am and what I am in day-to-day activity in life. Today I have an opinion of myself unlike that of previous years. I am more realistic about my actual existence, which is God-given." --- **Deborah Francis**

Congratulations! You're almost at the finish line. We hope by now that you are more of a DOER than just a READER.

With this course, you will get going only if you put into action everything you've learned. Reading alone is not good enough.

Your confidence will shoot high only if you are a doer; and on that note, let's kick off the last session.

****
The New Confident You!
****

Have you been putting into action all of the recommendations that you came across in this course?

If yes, we are glad that you are really serious about making a difference in your life by increasing your confidence levels and self-esteem. We trust that you are prepared to do an analysis of how you felt before and how you feel now.

We understand this could be challenging, arranging the thoughts without being subjective. But I bet you will feel great once you are done or at least relieved! And you know what? If you have come this far, you are already a champion.
Yes! You heard it right! CHAMPION!

You have taken the first step and you deserve to treat yourself. Go out and put into action what you have learned. Changing your bad habits and developing new productive habits is a treat in itself. Jot down all the things you have noticed that illustrate that your confidence is improving, no matter how small or large they are.

We will now give you an **8-point reminder** that will be a quick reference on how to get confidence in any given situation:

1. **Think through your desired outcome Ask yourself: "How would a person with confidence do this?"**

2. **Visualize yourself doing the tasks. Close your eyes and see yourself completing those projects successfully.**

3. **Prepare yourself thoroughly.**

4. **Before you begin any project, go through it in your mind several times and be positive.**

5. **Put everything into perspective. No matter what it is, will people really care about it in 20 years' time?**

6. **GET IT DONE!**

7. **Learn to accept the outcome—Everything is a learning experience.**

8. **REWARD yourself for DOING rather than TALKING about doing it!**

****

Well, here you are, ready to face the world with confidence as this book comes to a close. **You can do yourself a huge favor by reading this book again.**

We hope you have gained enough from this course to last you a lifetime. Remember, you only live once and hence, you have to make the most of every opportunity and every moment that comes your way. And every time someone tries to give a blow to your confidence, just remember what David Brinkley said:

"A successful person is one who can lay a firm foundation with the bricks that others throw at him or her."

All the best for a PROSPEROUS & CONFIDENT future!

YOU ARE UNDENIABLY CONFIDENT!!!

Notes

Notes

Notes

Hasheem Francis is the Co-founder and CEO of Built To Prosper Companies. With two decades of entrepreneurial and leadership experience, Hasheem Francis is a leadership consultant and advisor to CEOs, business leaders, corporate executives and community leaders across the country. His vast expertise in dealing with business change, along with his strong financial investment background and leadership development skills, enables him to provide unique and unparalleled counsel to a diverse range of industry professionals. **www.HasheemFrancis.com**

Deborah Francis is the Co-founder and COO of Built To Prosper Companies. Deborah is an entrepreneur, best-selling author, investor, keynote speaker, recognized industry thought leader, and an expert on business development. Deborah Francis has developed curriculum and delivered training sessions specifically related to entrepreneurship, small business development, and professional development. Deborah has trained, led and mentored hundreds of people with her functional knowledge and educational background. Deborah has an M.S. Ed. Masters in Secondary Education of English. **www.DeborahFrancisCompanies.com**

BUILT TO PROSPER
COMPANIES
Success is Created By Visionaries & Built By Leaders

Built To Prosper Companies

Hasheem Francis & *Deborah Francis*

Co Founder, CEO   Co Founder, COO

Consulting ▪ Investing ▪ Training

BUILT TO PROSPER
COMPANIES
"EMPOWERING BUSINESSES TO PROSPER"

Built To Prosper Companies is an innovative business network that provides strategic investments in a diverse portfolio of companies. As a leading provider of business consulting and training since 1999, Built To Prosper Companies has worked with over 1500 small to mid-sized businesses. ***Built To Prosper Companies specializes in business: planning, marketing, leadership development and raising business investment capital.***

Built To Prosper Companies is in business to produce value and unparalleled results for companies by delivering business solutions that support them in driving revenue growth. This is done with an uncompromising commitment toward serving our clients with the utmost in respect, integrity, and the highest standards of excellence. Our delivery model is predicated on exacting alignment with the unique aspects of each client's business strategy and organizational structure and culture, ensuring each client engagement provides clear and actionable tactics that will drive success on an ongoing, quantifiable basis. We believe that by delivering on this promise, we will help our clients not only drive incremental revenue growth, but also bring more meaning and fulfillment to our clients, their business, and the clients they serve. Built To Prosper Companies is headquartered in Orlando, FL, with affiliate operations in New York, NY, and Hilton Head, SC. ***For more information on how we can help your business, visit:***

www.BuiltToProsperCompanies.com.

Would You Like To Hire Professional Speakers, for your next event? We have a team of specialists who are experts in taking care of all our events and making sure we fully understand your needs as an organization. We have been producing amazing results for our clients and seminar participants for over a decade.

Our mission is to empower you and your team with the same tools and strategies that have been used to help millions of people from around the world take their lives to the next level. Your organization is on its way to learning some life-changing skills that will impact every aspect of your organization. *For booking, email: Info@BTPCompanies.com*.

Mentors help you excel to the next level. The Built To Prosper Mentoring Program *(Leadership, Wealth, Business, and Health)* remains the most comprehensive program of its kind and a leader's best choice for exceeding their maximum goals.

Our mentors specialize in giving you the latest techniques on how to become an effective leader, build a profitable business, amass wealth, and develop a healthy lifestyle. Your mentor will also instruct you on the most effective use of our proprietary materials and techniques. If you are serious about creating the life that you desire, it's time to get your own Built To Prosper Mentor. *For more information, visit: www.BTPMentoring.com.*

Built To Prosper Magazine was "Created By Visionaries And Built By Leaders." **Built To Prosper Magazine** emphasizes leadership and business development; it engages and addresses every aspect of an entrepreneur's life. This magazine provides a platform for entrepreneurs to express their passion for leadership, business, family, faith, finance, and health.

To order a copy of the fastest growing magazine, please visit: **www.BuiltToProsperMagazine.com.**

To advertise in Built To Prosper Magazine, email: **Info@BTPCompanies.com.**